JUST LIKE DADDY

Karen Elrod Dismukes

MINERVA PRESS

ATLANTA LONDON SYDNEY

JUST LIKE DADDY
Copyright © Karen Elrod Dismukes 1999

ISBN 0 75410 369 2

First Published 1999 by
MINERVA PRESS
315–317 Regent Street
London W1R 7YB

Printed in Great Britain for Minerva Press

JUST LIKE DADDY

To Magnolia,

from a wildly undisciplined writer,

and to my partner through life, who taught me to see life with optimism and who taught me the American work ethic. To Magnolia Chesterfield White North, my preacher and my teacher: she quoted the bible daily, she taught me to dance, drink, and play cards. Together we raised her ten children and my three. Between the two of us we had enough children to form the thirteen colonies. We had the Southern American experience. She is always there. Thank you Mag, I love you.

Acknowledgments, also, to my family who have been the diligent characters, forever staging and acting. Thank you to my two faithful friends Margaret Henson and Sarah Allen, who have listened to these stories in awe, in tears, in laughter, and who have become so much of this tragi-comedy theater that they sometimes magically appear on the stage themselves.

'Miz' Dismukes

Foreword

The South is howling and weeping. Americans need to be aware that there are subtle tragi-comic changes happening that will affect the world history books of the 'Great Democracy'. The topics are political, racial, religious and gender related. One should watch with obedient eyes. One should listen to the mountain's mumblings and the bayou's chants: they are shifting America, focusing in the South, a region at odds, either at random or by a literary howl from authors such as Karen Elrod Dismukes. The South is an American problem, and deep within it lie universal solutions.

Karen Elrod Dismukes has chosen to present problems in the simplest form of literary jargon. Yet the reader will be seduced by her four-way stops at personalities that range from the honorable judge in a small town, to Magnolia's spirituality at 'the fuen' (funeral). There are electrifying emotional surges that give the reader a sense of pathos. There are problems of generational strife that remain unresolved. There are pointed rebukes at the Southern aristocracy, who still around in the 1990s, which make reference to the Southern family tradition; the rigid ways that never acceded back to the union; not unlike Mistral's social stew in Provencal.

Miss Dismukes addresses complexity with a simplicity that allows any reader to laugh, to cry, to become angry, or to disbelieve. Karen Elrod Dismukes sometimes offends the reader with words that are too truthful and too raw.

Preface

Oddly enough, I am taking a course in fiction writing because my poetry has become very prosaic. I am fifty years old and have been writing poetry since I was nineteen. Writing is my decision-making process, my relationship, my direct path to a satisfying destination. So, in reality who am I?

I am the owner of a $7 m. ladies' clothing business that I inherited, in name only, from my grandparents. My grandmother was from Baxter, Tennessee, which is seventy-nine miles south-west of Nashville. She was also a working woman of the 1890s; a designer of hats for the millinery department of Mr. Jon in New York City. My grandfather was a stable, entrepreneurial man from Cookville, Tennessee. After eighty years of prosperity their business suffered the same gentle loss as many other Southern businesses; businesses that still maintained standards in quality of merchandise and service, while the owners and their families lived on cash flow instead of profits. These families lived in the Southern eloquence and opulence of columned mansions and chauffeur-driven cars. They believed that they belonged to some grand fraternal order that kept them at debutante balls and private schools. They believed that this unreality kept them inexhaustibly wealthy. Indeed, they had forgotten the work ethic that replaced such hierarchies, and some Church of Christ members, converted to Methodism, had a bit more standing in the eyes of God Almighty, who blessed them every Sunday as they lost profits unabashedly and sang innocently 'Abide With Me'.

I am now married to a retired colonel in the army who took over my business upon his retirement. We have expanded our sales to all parts of the United States, via three hundred shows a year.

We have three children. A daughter who graduated from Hollins College, VA. She is a French major and a marathon runner and now lives in Holland. Our second daughter attends Prescott College in Arizona and majors in photography, and minors in outdoor education. I am very proud of her photographic work. She and I are admirers of Mapplethorpe, Arbis and Mann. I do not think art is pornographic and I do not believe in censorship for the arts. My son attends Montgomery Bell Academy as a senior and after many years of living his father's dreams as a football player, he has won All District and All Metro awards. In addition, he has won two art awards, one state and one national in art 101. His yin and yang must have united to please his mother and his father before leaving for Ole Miss or Vanderbilt as a 1993 freshman. He has no desire to play football again.

I have an interest in travel, having traveled extensively in the Caribbean, and have had thoughts of living on my own island, or restoring a house in the south of France where I have spent the last three summers.

I have spent the majority of my other forty summers in the vicinity of the University of the South in Monteagle Sunday School Assembly, which is similar to Chataugua, NY. I hope to take the writer's course at the university this summer.

My education has consisted of attending Florida Southern, Middle Tennessee State University and several correspondence courses; the latest under Tom McKeown at the University of Wisconsin.

I have had about twenty poems published by Californian publishers. I have no interest in seeing my name in bold print, or listening to poetry being read to chamber music again, the culmination and realization of that was when I was invited to read poetry in New York with Sid Caesar, whom I thought was deceased, and when I received a coffee mug reading 'Best Poet in the Year'.

I am a keen tennis player, I enjoy hunting and fishing and I like to think that I can canoe. Entomology is a subject that I remain interested in.

William Faulkner, Adrienne Rich, Walt Whitman, Mona van Doynne, Elizabeth Bishop, and Sylvia Plath are a few of my favorites. Joseph Brodsky and Marguerite Duras are of interest and perhaps have been influential to me.

Karen Elrod Dismukes

Contents

Part One

Broken Bye-Lo

You have heard of the circus freak and you have heard of the china doll under glass. Well, ever since i broke my mother's doll, one that her mother gave her in 1923, i have been a freak in the circus.

Now my mother is a royal bitch, putting on airs of being rich and proper: graduate of Gunston Hall in Washington DC and mother of five children whose father, despite being an alcoholic, was an aristocrat. i guess you might have called him that, back in the 1930s.

You see, he was religious and intellectual and went through bleak, dreary times with the light of Christ. He went to church once a year and trembled, paying some price for his disgraceful condition, but knowing that he needed some space for his soul to expand.

i even saw the stained glass edge away from its lead when he entered the church with his ninety year old father (Daddy was sixty-five). The little blues of Christ's head would become distanced from Christ himself.

The furthest thing from my mind was my mother and how sorry i was that i broke her doll.

My mother sat in the front row all frilled and coiffed, as people in the South did in the Fifties, and my daddy and his father sat in those pews at back (Grandfather sat straighter than Father), smelling of their toddies of black Jack Daniel's, or maybe green label (one was better than the other), and i was embarrassed that i had to sit with a successfully liturgical mother, even though she could not spell liturgy if you asked her to look it up in *Webster's*.

i would glance back at Daddy during the Christmas twilight service and know that he and his father believed in lighting candles but only at formal dinners, and that it had nothing to do with passing on the light.

My daddy, leaning on his father, would quietly move out of the church without anyone knowing they had been there except me, and the ushers who helped them out. Then the chauffeur would help them into the car and drive a block down Main Street to where they lived, and then my mother and her children, like a brood of chickens, would peck and prance their way out.

On the night of the Savior's birth.

Me, with candle tallow dripped all over my coat and repenting broken china, and my brothers and sisters followed Mother Hen, condemning Daddy for all of his worthlessness and probably thinking that Santa Claus would not come if they were not in bed straight after church and that he was, in fact, my mother in drag. Santa, in my family was a man, you know, so how could these children think that Mama could give them anything? So Santa, in drag, came and we had a dreadful Christmas morning receiving only things we needed and not extravagant gifts.

Then we would go to Daddy's and get color TVs and children's Touch-Tone princess telephones and footballs and tennis balls and tennis rackets from Australia and doll's houses that imitated houses on Main Street. Daddy now lived with his daddy, one block down, and Grandfather 'caretaker' gladly rushed in for my daddy and it made Mama look bad.

Women didn't have a chance in those days when there were people like Daddy who had a daddy to take care of him.

i asked my mother last year, 'What is a freak?'

She said, 'Remember when i used to take you to the state fair and the circus in Nashville, those deformed people in cages and fat, *fat* ladies?' (double fat because she has gotten a little fatter herself now), 'Those are freaks.'

i said, 'Daddy was a freak in those tails and bow ties?'

She said, 'Darling, your father was a perfect gentleman, have you forgotten?'

i guess i am just like Daddy.

But i didn't forget when i was five, that i broke her china doll.

i wonder if Daddy knew that china broke so easily, and whether Mama really loved china, and if she really thought those were freaks and that he looked great in bow ties.

Well, My Grandmother Had a Lot More To Do Than Take Care of Daddy in 1913

She had business to attend to.

Bless his heart; he tossed and rolled and tumbled at the age of three. He wanted his daddy and his mom, of course, who were at the bus-i-ness.

The world allows one to think that someone else is engaged or full of activity that has nothing to do with a crying baby, unless that is your business; bus-i-ness.

So Daddy cried until his little soul became almost independent.

He rose to walk and stumbled and realized that no one would help him, so he made up a formula.

i think Daddy was smart.

He observed a wasps' nest that multiplied outside the window once, starting with a little nest, a little piece of paper that God just secreted down in his hand with a pencil, and he looked at its vastness and its surroundings, and took the old unpainted rocking chair on the front porch that became a rocking chair on the porch of a Victorian mansion when he was sixteen.

He had on lace collars and buckled shoes that hurt his feet, but they were the best, with brass buckles and all, and he was probably still making that list, but he had a real pen now and even an eraser in case he made a mistake.

My daddy did not like to make mistakes because he was now well educated; he had been to military school in Georgia and was just home for the summer.

Well, i bet he had that same vision of a wasp who had started with one cell or unit and now had a bigger home than where he used to live. i bet he watched those wasps every day and patterned his whole life out of perfection.

He observed the short life of a mother who gives birth to children and never takes back; just keeps building, and i bet he thought he owned that nest and a lot of others and his plan was to have a lot, just like that mother wasp.

He made a plan to open a telecommunications station, that is a radio station, and own a plantation with lots of servants and he probably waved that paper like the flag of independence.

Then his mother said he had to go to college.

Well, that could be fun, he had a new Coupe de Ville and all of that and he was plenty smart.

So he forgot all about the wasps' nest and the organized plan and became the charmer of the Beta fraternity in 1924. He was not very fraternal to his tantrum-throwing sister who always wore taffeta and could never get a date because she was so mad all the time at her mama and daddy for having 'Daddy'.

So they used to go to the cotillion and pretend they were not brother and sister. Daddy didn't care because they had the biggest car and there were a lot of cute girls who were nice and did not act like his sister.

So he forgot his plan and the wasp nest and the paper he was writing on, except for one sunny breezy day when he was sixteen and was on the front porch in a stiff white wicker chair. He remembered how hurtful it had been to see that one wasp, in her golden brilliance, struggle and gnaw and make a home for so many others. She always was regal and busy.

Then someone called from the rose garden and said, 'Mister Cecil your guests are here.' And he almost ran through the back porch screen to get to the freshly rolled tennis court, which his father had objected to his building, and, because he had been thinking, he took out that little silver flask and took a wet drink.

Then, like Nijinsky, he danced on to the tennis court and won. He was naturally graceful, i guess he got that from watching the mother wasp, who with all her duty still remained beautiful…

Well, Daddy forgot his dreams and had a sharp memory of reality when World War II started.

Daddy, remember, you can't come home again.

He was probably just like that queen wasp who kept those little units going until everyone had a home.

What Am I Doing This For?

'Bluebirds can fly. Why can't i?' asked my father in 1943.

'Bluebirds can fly. Why can't i?' i asked myself in 1993.

We both loved Judy Garland.

i am a humanist and a spiritualist.

My family approved so i married him.

i drank champagne, rode tractors and bought our butler's truck.

i stopped writing and started a thriving business.

i had three children three years apart.

They told me to do these things because it was normal.

'Just like your father, you are just like your father,' everyone told me.

Well, he wasn't normal.

Of course my father has been dead for twenty years.

He had wonderful midnight conversations and became so obnoxious to his friends that they would never call any more.

He even wrote the script for news articles and TV shows, in between gin and tonics, and had little scribbles of papers and lists for each person; lawyers and doctors and newspaper owners.

Daddy started the first radio station in the state of Tennessee right after the war, i think. It was 1945.

He was also a coward.

He graduated from Georgia military academy and was afraid to go to summer camps of any kind.

Then the war started.

His father had a brother killed in World War I and had received the Legion of Merit or the Purple Heart, or something they gave for being brave.

Grandmother knew she had really goofed – judged the future incorrectly.

That is what had happened: sending Daddy off to a military school and making him look handsome in that great uniform and a private in Sherman's town.

She never thought there would be another war or that he would ever have to go to a real war.

i think her father was a coward too, because his picture always hung above the mantel in her bedroom and she loved the way he looked in that old gold gilded frame. She always told me he had weak eyes.

She had weak eyes too, which meant they could not see the future too well.

They were object–comfort related. They also had grandiose ideas and were very creative.

Well, back to the coward in the military, my daddy, in World War II. The secretary of state was Cordell Hull, who just happened to be my grandmother's cousin. So he and President Roosevelt put together this idea that there should be a radar station in South America to receive messages neutral to the war which was being fought on the European continent.

i would imagine that the secretary of state had a little of that Tennessee creativity in him, as well.

At this point he was probably very charming, with his handsomeness and Southern gentlemaness, to President Roosevelt, so they did this for Daddy.

He went to Brazil to fight the war.

In the meantime i was born to an ill-fated marriage that ultimately killed him with his gin bottles.

i probably killed him being the oldest and all, and marrying a military man who reminded him of all of his cowardliness and such. My husband loved and hated my father; that's the way it is sometimes.

Then Daddy went to Brazil for three years and played tennis for all those South Americans and, while winning, performed a ballet with his graceful form to much applause. They thought he was a Diaghilev or a Nijinsky.

i was stuck in the United States until i was three, with my beauty queen mother and a grandmother who really loved me but was a hypochondriac.

Well, i will skip through a few years because they say i am just like Daddy.

Bluebirds can fly. Why can't i?

Indian Money

Crinoid limestone, fragments of stems of encrinites in middle-Triassic stone.

Free swimming marine animals.

Well i guess it is all Indian money.

We were taught Indian money by our parents who used to take us all the time on little picnics near a creek.

The difficulty really was finding the right spot and view. i have forgotten the other requirements, but there were some, like it was the basket that didn't have the proper glasses, and we didn't have matching silver and this was not the ideal place.

The children had always collected crinoid limestone from Tennessee. We thought we were finding money like panning for gold or silver, i guess. So we were sent off, one child following the other, hunting for crinoids.

If the parents are making love on the grass, it had to be a special place or we would not have taken such a long time to find the ideal spot or all of that Indian money in the creek of the riverbeds.

And the children came back too soon and they had a leader, like in *Lord of the Flies*, who knew nothing but was the oldest child and in control.

We were probably scared, and they probably cared, like the movie, *Splendor in the Grass*.

i, the oldest, showed respect and they have relied on me ever since, or 'every sense'.

We laugh now, sitting at the kitchen table, at my brother who was so scared because he thought Mama and Daddy were dead and the Indians had laid them on top of one another in pyramid form.

Just like Daddy told me about the Indians who once lived in our region.

And i probably told the other five, and we believed it, and thought Indians would come out of the trees and put us on top of one another and then we would be dead and alive at the same time, because they didn't wake up after we came back the third time from finding Indian money.

We had some other picnics where i really found the largest crinoid, or whatever we called limestone Indian money, and i knew it was the chief's money, and i went back and said to Daddy, 'Don't worry anymore, i can find money, i am like the chief.'

The funny thing is that he believed me and he knew i was only six.

We had this other older chief called
Pop. E.

When the time came, he turned the grand order over to me.

So Daddy just kept taking us on picnics and having the proper Victorian order and having nice things at hand.

They relied on me to be the mother and the father and i had the power of the conch, like Ralph (you might know who he is if you have read *Lord of the Flies*, now required reading at school), and i knew i did not have Piggy's glasses; the real thing that would start a fire.

But we all lived for two other generations, no truth being told.

i don't want to sound like what ever his name is, oh, like Jesse Jackson or like Zora Hurston. Their eyes are watching God, no interpretation, *no problem, mon*.

We are the children of the world, which leads me to another story about Sunday School and a song we used to sing about the children of the world. i thought they were all alike, colored, red, yellow, black or white, that really could be an incorrect way to see all the children of the world.

Swimming Lessons

Have i ever told you about the breaststroke?

Well, i took swimming lessons when i was five years old and they were with this Olympic swimmer in Tennessee, Molly McKnight.

She was really neat, i thought, until she made me try the breaststroke.

Well, my mama had always told me that you don't look at naked people; i guess it was Southern modesty, and you don't stare at people and you especially don't look at parts of their bodies.

By five, i had decided these were sacred parts, or that they went with marriage, or had something to do with having babies, and so when this Olympic instructor said, 'Do the breaststroke', i thought it was something very wrong.

Does she want us to swim above water and stroke our breasts?

My mama told me that was not nice.

i could swim on my back and swim under water and do right and left breaths, but i just couldn't do the breaststroke.

i just didn't have any breasts.

i thought they were of no use, except for feeding babies in Africa and other deprived countries where they didn't have Carnation milk and sterilizers and bottles and maids.

(i learned later that some women used them to attract men.)

So i just could not understand the breaststroke.

i liked my instructor real well, she was so different and all and spoke like a Bostonian.

i asked her how i might accomplish the breaststroke, and she told me that if i could go under water and hold my breath and act like a frog then i could do the stroke, kind of like when people are exercising at the country club and doing jumping jacks, which i never understood either. But i used to play 'Mother may i' on the sidewalk and do scissors steps, so i could do this breaststroke.

Well, i went underwater with full force and i came up humming like a frog, and the only way i could swim was if i remembered the breaststroke and looked like a frog on a lily pad in a prone position; ready to move if the enemy came.

Then my arms and legs came together and i had this sensational feeling of grace and I could swim and it had nothing to do with my undeveloped breasts.

i was just on my stomach in the Stones River swimming pool doing the breaststroke that took pectoral muscles.

A Southern Memory

i have this friend i sometimes have coffee with except now we have changed to herbal tea.

Her name is Rebecca: and it's like she and i have interfaced in the past but she went on.

Anyway, my friend and i were discussing dolls. i hated dolls when i was growing up and she loved them. She used to make up a whole family out of her dolls.

Well, i had a sister and i hated her dolls too, but we always had to play dolls, so i cut Sparkle Plenty's hair and painted Toni Doll's cheeks with red paint and broke the china dolls.

i think, psychologically, it was not an accident, but i sure got a lot of whippings with my mother's blue plastic hairbrush.

Well, my friend and i were talking about ironing ladies (they were Negroes), and by my recollection it was a great honor to get to drive this big old Packard to Vine Street and pick up the ironing, and sometimes take the ironing, at age sixteen.

It was a kind of power trip to be in the projects with all these blacks and arrive in a big car and pay Dorothy $1.75 for a whole basket of beautiful sheets and shirts and blouses and i think even dresses for the younger ones.

Well, my bonus and compensation was controlling money and power trips, but my friend said her mother always picked up the ironing, and one day her mother went on the wrong day and all of these little pickaninnies, which i think is what my grandmother called them, had on Miss Rebecca's clothes and her sister's clothes.

The ironing lady was really embarrassed that she was letting her children wear the clothes in between laundries, and my friend said her mother was so disgusted, she said, 'Keep the damn clothes, i am not having my lily whites wear those clothes after Negroes have worn them.' And she had to go to the commissary, all the way to Jackson, Miss., and buy all new clothes for her children.

Then they wondered why the colonel's check bounced at the commissary the next week, and the colonel berated his wife and said she could do her own damned ironing like a wife should do instead of showing off in front of all his superiors, and she begged him for $1.75 to get the ironing done (she was Southern and she didn't have a clue how to iron). He said, 'Hell no,' it would put her in her place instead of reading all of those trashy books by Pearl Buck. And Rebecca said she cried for nine days and then her mother just said 'Okay,' and sold the family heirlooms, like oak tables and horsehair benches.

Then she found a secret ironing lady. This one was white and she fell in love with her. This ironing lady's name was Elizabeth, and finally Rebecca's mother started taking the ironing everyday and staying at Elizabeth's while the ironing was being done. Anything to escape the verbal badgering of Rebecca's father.

Elizabeth took in ironing because she was a hippie from the Sixties, and believed in communal living and played the guitar; songs like 'Send in the Clowns' and 'Michael Rowed the Boat Ashore', and Rebecca's mother came home happy after going to the ironing lady who became her lover.

Later on, when Elizabeth could no longer sing or iron and was on a respirator at the community hospital with some disease all over her body, so they said, Rebecca's family would find their mother sitting holding Elizabeth's hand, which she did until the day she died.

Rebecca's mother said those were the best five years of her life: visiting Elizabeth with the ironing and making silk screen peace signs while she listened to Judy Collins. She even came home and sang 'Will the Circle Be Unbroken?'.

Rebecca's mother was now wearing jeans and went braless and pulled her unruly curly hair up in a bandanna.

Ironing days can give people a lot of joy and power.

The catharsis was that Rebecca's mother even published a little book entitled *The Circle Will Not Be Unbroken We're Just Passerbys* by the ironing lady.

(Of course, she used a pseudonym so her husband wouldn't know about her happiness.)

Lavada

What was it Lavada really wanted?

She was twenty-five years old last October and still had no real future plans.

Her attention span was about as long as the flotation record of a helium balloon.

She had fought her way through Nashville's best private high school.

She had traveled two continents, extensively and dangerously.

She had a master of arts degree from a prestigious avant-garde college.

She preferred living in tents, hiking, fishing and white water rafting to normal domestication.

'Normal', by her mother's definition, was a collection of big old nineteenth-century houses; houses her mother loved and cared for and which were heavily decorated with generational antiques. And yet, now that she was back in South Carolina living with a man who was possibly the choice of her future, she phoned her mother daily, often finding her in the mountain retreat where she preferred to stay until the winter had moved in and the cold iced her breath as she blew little ringlets of smoke from her cigarettes, which showed frozen fringes on their poisoned air. Her mother showed a preference for slow suicide.

Yes, she taunted her mother every morning; with every phone call, she recalled her past.

How could she ever have a wedding with her broken memories?

Who would choose a life like that to live?

Could there even be choice in Lavada's life?

She had guided white-water rafting, she had taken modern dance, she had thrown pots, yet her real love was photography.

But she herself could not see or tolerate the details of reality that etched each creation, the smears of scarred nothingness that came out in blurred Polaroid transfers, the reminder that there was no black and white as her negatives printed the very contradiction without the pain, that there were few choices even in retrospect; life for Lavada was a pedagogic procession of antiquated teachings.

Yes, she could be a photographer and crouch behind a lens catching life at the wrong moments, recording the tragedy of the lack of childhood happiness.

She could use automatic flashes to turn their ailing and aged companion Magnolia into a brilliantly white 'north' star.

Magnolia, who had lived with them and caused them to leave Gs off the end of their words, like swingin' and singin'.

People would always know she was Southern by her speech.

She could even go to color prints, and enlarge them into modern life-size figures,

but these photographic scribes could never capture the hurt they felt when their mother had taken Lavada, and her brother and sister, Christmas caroling with a group of neighborhood children and their parents.

They had a wonderful time singing 'O' Christmas Tree' and leaving the houses with 'We Wish You a Merry Christmas'.

Then she had taken them home to the big house, and their father, in one of his rages, which stemmed from army life, all his life, and small town, Southern Baptist mentality, which he could never elude, threw a butcher's knife at their mother and broke Jack Daniel's bottles in the sink and threw the silver eggnog cups at the lavishly set table for thirty-two Christmas guests.

Oh, how she had wished for Magnolia's warm low-slung breasted body to hold her until they stopped fighting, but Lavada remembered that night for more reasons than those crushing memories.

It was the only night the 'fury' had overwhelmed their mother. She had commanded them, not in her gentle or sometimes random tone, tainted by having sipped a bit too much wine with her friends, but had commanded them, like a general, to go to their rooms, and promised that Santa would have their stockings filled by the morning.

They obeyed and went up the spiraled dark mahogany staircase that rose to black oblivion even though they hated going upstairs by themselves; they hated this house because it was 'historic' and all their friends talked about the ghosts in it.

The next morning, Magnolia was the one who told them their father had lived a life without caution, and that their mother was too headstrong, but was clearly a gentle woman.

But it was Christmas, and Magnolia told them to look on the mantel at the wonderful filled stockings. Then she put on her Christmas uniform of black with a little white lace cap and apron. Then she told them they had to go with their grandfather for a while. But Lavada wanted Mama to wake up so she could open her presents.

But Magnolia put our coats on over our robes and L.D., the chauffeur, picked us up to go to Grandfather's, who lived only a block away.

She should have known she would never see her father again.

We would never see our father again and again and again.

Lavada changed her name; it was Catherine. She went west for two years, living recklessly and dangerously.

Why did she come back to roots?

There was an unforeseen silence that might give her the faith that her mother's way was right, she was better off. He was dead.

But with all the modern-day therapy she had been through, and the medicine she had taken, she still had blackouts when the father's body whispered to hers inside. Even through the lithium she always heard him say, 'I love you.'

Maybe Rand Butler Rutledge could save her. Could she give herself freely to love? Could she lay alongside and run her fingers through Butler's long golden locks? Could they, with abandon, romp through clover fields and make daisy chains, like young lovers in storybooks?

Maybe their children would never know the blank spaces of her photography if it were put away for ever.

Maybe Lavada could have a life if her mother accidentally forgot the missing scenes, forgot her cigarettes, left her unfinished books unwritten, and if her mother, herself, smoldered in the ashes of one of those burned-out houses she had always loved.

She would be the past, unsure that Lavada would remember the end of the rhyme,

'Ashes, ashes, we all fall down.'

Maybe that would be all she remembered of the child's game played so spontaneously; happiness without meaning.

Ring around the rosy
Pocket full of posy
Ashes, ashes, we all fall down

The First Hunt In October
'The Child is Father of the Man'

The boy moved sheepishly along the wall where his hunting guns were sat like dominos in a handmade cherry gun cabinet. The man who made the cabinet was dead.

The boy's dad had bought the cabinet at an auction.

He had also bought the man's boots and Stetson hats.

His dad had called the man a 'playboy', a 'party guy', a 'character'; someone who always played the game of life in ways that were bigger than life itself.

The boy even remembered his father saying that the dead man's father should have his son 'exterminated'.

The boy's room had hunting trophies, antique furniture, unwanted appointments, like a Chinese roof tile made into a lamp, fishing equipment, a collection of baseball cards, and a closet full of polo shirts.

As he edged along the wall of his room he felt anger at the expectations his father had of him, and his two sisters. How football, sororities, fraternities and the Junior League had been his father's main concern. Yet he remembered that when his mother had arranged for his father to become a member of the Rotary Club and the Chamber of Commerce and a member of the business steering committee of their city, his father had flatly refused. His father said his work was 'too important' to join in community service. The boy thought this was very contradictory.

How poisonous the boy's whole lifestyle had been to the development of his soul.

He reached into the gun cabinet and felt his hand move along the smooth stock of his newly purchased Beretta twelve gauge. Aloud, he said to himself, as if he were talking to someone else in the room, 'This will be an easy hunt.'

It was such a natural feeling to have this pounding in his heart, thinking about the trophy he might bring home.

He had a lingering self-image of his calm face.

He was everybody's friend.

He believed in right and wrong, yet his real personality was camouflaged behind expensive props and misinterpreted script. There had to be a way to refuse the payoffs for reality; the reality he could see.

His father lay in deep depression, watching boxing matches on the television in the master bedroom. Shortly, his father would board a plane going to New York. The boy would then be happy.

His mother was cuddled up on the couch upstairs, with a blank gaze on her face. Too much scotch and soda. Occasionally she would rise, go to her desk and type lines of poetry.

His sisters' rooms were empty. They had made a getaway: one to the European continent and the other to the river working as a guide – the great Colorado river nurturing her soul.

His dad called her a 'river rat'.

Why was he left to make the final break? Why was he the head hunter?

He was still left to the risk of fulfilling someone else's life. Yet he had come home with all the trophies.

He really believed in catch and release on fishing trips.

There was a sense of involvement in the catch and a sense of freedom in controlling or preserving the universe in release.

Now, he automatically switched the gun shells into the barrel of the gun. As he moved through the house he felt this was not such an easy hunt after all.

This animal was the most helpless of any he had ever hunted. It was a still target.

Finally, the pain of the lonely house reached the mind's eye, like a filmmaker focusing for the last shot.

There was the brilliance of sunlight that gave the target enough screenplay. There was no dialogue like the silent movies of long ago.

All the matched colored fabric in his father's room; turned black and white. For a moment the film clicked like it was broken and then there was the loud roar as if the MGM lion was beginning the movie. There were no previews or cartoons, just the loud sound of the king of beasts.

The reality moved into a red drip along monogrammed bed covers.

At last there was freedom. There was no more fear.

The clearness of this picture was so real.

The film was over and the boy could become the real artist, not the actor. This was not just screen play.

He took his twelve gauge and jauntingly walked out the door to the terrace.

There were beautiful flowers he had never noticed.

There were dying tomato plants his father had planted in his mother's geranium bed.

Every image was red for a moment; tomatoes, geraniums, impatiens and a memory.

His black Labrador waited for him patiently as he carelessly laid his gun across the chaise longue. He and his dog turned toward a country lane for retrieval practice. He would win the dog trials tomorrow, he was sure. He was favored in the race.

He would also move the last trophy to the farm tomorrow.

The only difference between this trophy and all the rest was that it would not hang on the wall. Almost like catch and release.

No one would even ask where his father had gone.

He felt a sense of freedom and happiness. There was a little creased smile on his lips.

He had a picture on the wall in his room of his father as a paratrooper. This would hold the image of a trophy until Christmas.

His father was always gone until December.

Then he might tell someone about this hunt.

Trilogy

Trilogy, by Webster's definition, is a set of three related plays, novels, etc. which together form an extended, unified work, though each has its own unity. This chapter was named 'Trilogy', by Ms Dismukes, as she looked through family albums and was caught by the body language of the photo that provides the cover for the chapter. The father appears as the godhead sitting casually with his two children.

The black and white photo hints of unification.

As the reader examines the vignettes in the chapter, 'Trilogy', he may reach a different conclusion. Outward looks or external appearances and internal emotions often are diabolically opposed. It is often discovered in closer examination that body language gives the family picture a very sad ending.

I

Katherine has a chubby but firm arm around her father's shoulder that dwarfs him. He looks as unprepared for two little girls wrapped around his body as he did when he was called to war.

He was also as unprepared for love as he was for war.

Katherine has a death grip, one that she has inherited by primogeniture. Leadership qualities are expected by her creator, her father.

The lace pinafore is a Queen Victoria-like robe – she passes for royalty.

II

The Creator is described throughout the book – he is merely a prototype in the picture to show that he exists. He leaves all living to others, although he exists in form. He has a sense of *Great Gatsby* style. His presence cannot be dismissed. He is perhaps demonic in appearance. He has already made a Faustian pact with the Devil.

III

The second child in the trilogy looks a bit like Mary Magdalene, but is in reality victimized as the second child. She experiences the resurrection with every moment because her only means of survival is martyrdom and obscurity of reality – the real details of living.

She performs for the father, is a Christ figure for her mother, manipulates herself through sacrifice and dies of anemia. There is no blood sacrifice left to contribute. She is crucified by the older sister, lacks a father's remission of sins, and stays in a cave after death; the stone is not rolled away – she is a tragic figure, martyred neither for cause nor sainthood, and never knowing why.

Ol' Possum Plays Dead
Or Don't Tell a Southerner You Treed a Possum

When i was little i heard the older people talk about the possum or the ol' possum, they never said it correctly.

Or maybe it was the way i heard it because of a burst eardrum when i was three, or because of whatever Scott did to me that caused a tonsillectomy, and on top of that my (add, no adds, i think you spell that adenoids) were removed and i had to stay an extra week in the hospital and missed one half of the first grade, which i was able to make up in one month.

(My husband, before he was my husband, recognized this about me right away.)

i was socially promoted in my small town in 1970.

But, anyway, i couldn't hear very well, certain syllables were difficult, and when they took the retarded children out to test them for picking their noses in class because it was offensive, though i didn't think picking your nose was so bad if your mother had not given you a Kleenex, anyway, i had to go along with the retarded children, and i was so happy when they tried to see if i could hear any better after Daddy's friend, Dr. Scott, probably ruined my ears in a drunken stupor with his new instrument from Sears, because he had millions of dollars, but stayed in a very austere office, i know possums play dead.

i always heard this story about Dr. Scott finding a baby on his door step on Christmas Eve. He said it was the Christ Child, so he convinced his wife, who drank a lot of gin, that they should take this Christ Child in to live with them.

They named him Scott and he grew up to be normal, but he did not look like what i thought Christ should look like; as he got older he even looked like Dr. Scott, i thought.

Of course, nobody ever cared what i thought.

Ol' possums play dead.

i was just three or six maybe, but anyway, one day there was a big book in what we called our library, and i saw people lookin' in this book and arguing over a word my daddy had used on the news on his own radio station.

They said the word was 'adjunct'.

Well, i thought that sounded fine,

except the newspaper publisher said 'adjunct' was incorrect in the context; so i knew that book had something in it of value.

i had never seen a possum since my mother said we lived in town, that's because we lived on Main Street, so i looked in that book for possum and i looked for three days, at intervals, but i could never find that word.

So when i went back to school i asked my teacher if she ever heard of a possum, she said 'Yes', her dad used to kill them and they'd have possum stew.

'Well, how would you spell possum?' i asked.

She told me in the South we mispronounced it, it was o-possum; i should look under o-possum and i asked her why people just couldn't speak correctly. Maybe it was my hearing problem or maybe they weren't as well educated, or maybe the children always stayed with Negroes and they didn't always use the same dialect.

Well i couldn't wait to get home and look up o-possum, but it was not very exciting because the animal was wild and could hang by its tail and was ugly.

So then, i looked up 'adjunct' and read:

'adjunct' – '*a nonessential addition, component, teacher, confederate*', something about comradery or ally, and that was exactly right, in that Daddy had said Brazil was an adjunct to the United States in World War II.

There was a lot of adding to that statement and a lot of junk i could have added, too, about my mother crying in her bedroom at night when she thought i was asleep, and sobbing about another Southern gentleman who had a Portuguese baby he left in Brazil.

But i was three or five and i was to be seen, not heard.

At fifty i still can't tell the whole story
i know about life in the South.
O-possums play dead.
Don't ever tell a Southerner you treed a possum.

The Intimations of Dutch Life

It was October, as the team of Holland won over England the trees turned orange, and the tulips turned orange, and the beer turned from an amber fizz to orange juice with one hundred proof added. 'Banaen' became orange, and the peace palace turned into a huge mobile chariot, a pumpkin with Anheuser-Bush work horses pulling the entire team through the world shouting 'Viva la Holland'; 'Vers' 'Vriendelijk' 'Voodelig.'

Now i live at Dankerstratt, my name is Karin which means grace, beauty, purity. i have a daughter whose name is Tara; gone with the wind. Tara, meaning a mighty fortress, a standing structure of elegance and fortitude. i don't know how we select these names at birth, but they are given and stay with us until we die, and afterwards, in death and beyond because we are then engaged in a funeral or are burned ashes and have our names engraved upon an urn; so *purity* and *fortitude* start on a venture with the Wegdams' plural; they have long wonderful biblical and Catholic names that have ninety-five to a thousand letters in them, but they use nicknames like Ben and Ricki.

They are glowing, responsive, cordial people that love in an ordinary way or become very excitable about events such as their country being painted orange by simultaneous events such as victory in football and the autumn season.

We all have funny syllables or too many syllables in our names, at the moment. If i became baptized again i think i would use one letter and then it could mean anything and stand alone on any street and be a beginning and an end and become invisible if i should so choose, and i could simply be eyes without a body; sort of like authentic freedom.

But since i am on the street, shouting with everyone about orange, i have to wear my polo shirt and gabardine blazer and live in prison for a while longer as a multifaceted emblem behind bars, shouting and playing with the rest of the world.

Some day i will take my fortress and move to a very high mountain and engage with reality with Degeléis, my Capricorn, my pigmy goat, who will provide me with milk and cheese and we will sing melodies for the almighty who has made us self-sufficient.

Another Big House: In Holland

It is of Dutch style with a lovely color of porch-green and lots of ornamentation. i might look from the large windows that rattle with the rain every morning and see a hazy mirage of personality that i call 'me'. But i also might see the back buildings with petite gardens and a meter by meter balcony designed by the Surenam owner of this building, who has the ambitions of grand Dutch merchants and the architectural design vision of Van Gogh after his fifth nervous breakdown; yes, i do see the Surenam, Rans.

i leaned against the lead pipe rail on my first visit to the balcony and almost died. That is, i fell, after romantically leaning with my Chablis against the imaginary wrought iron, balancing in midair, like i didn't weigh one hundred and sixty-five pounds. i grasped for the fire escape that did not exist and then took a full parachute-style jump and landed back in the kitchen on the gas stove like the blonde witch who came to boil 'Hutspot', 'Haring' and 'Witte Brood' with a Spanish mask on that hides all of my dismay with the Dutch Halloween.

i have good will for this country; an abnormal investment of pleasure. i love their sense of balance, gained from maneuvering bicycles down narrow straats and the circulation of old legs peddling out of tradition and necessity.

Having drunk sherry and beer for breakfast, lunch, and dinner, they bike for miles to market, backpack their purchases for the day and then bike back home for ten kilometers, still laughing and making pleasure of what we Americans might call a dreadful day at the market.

i love this flat that i am sharing in the Gravenhage with my children who only want to please me. They are like the precious bluets that bloom on the window sill. The house has some flavor of Provence and Dutch and Grandmother's early American, eclectic chairs. There are funny memories of 1150 East Main Street, Tennessee, and i caress the familiar things like a photo album flashback. This afternoon i am going visiting to the architect who is building everything on the second floor and lives presently in the attic.

The Drear

It is gray, and smoke-filled and psychological and 12 Celsius and no heat, and drafts hover over my teacup to make ice cubes, and winds blow from the north sea reminding me of fairy-tale winds with huffy puffy faces.

There is no fireplace in this fifteenth-century building, there are little oriental gardens that are frozen on rooftops, and we love dried flowers because in the cold real flowers can't live.

We wear boots and layers of sweaters and imagine there is something spiritual about the breath that blows fog rings through the typewriter screen.

Somehow i love Holland for its attitude towards work because i can be cold and have the right to my imagination, and i can be in America and have every thought process sugarcoated with society's ideas.

i have to write with punctuation and i never hear real laughter from rosy-cheeked children like the ones who ride their bicycles in the rain and laugh with real witticism, accepting the cold and the cobblestone streets and that life is in the arrangement of one's head and is more existential.

Existence in reality is like the neighbor who freely sings a Surenam love song after vomiting from some viral infection that will always be with her since her episode with malnutrition in childhood and her little sexual moans that fill three stories of fifteenth-century buildings like little moans of ghosts that make music when all is drear.

The sun is a swift memory bank like the blending of the French Provencal fabric with forever flowers splashed on a lawn-green background. These flowers are without stems but have bright bright heads that are always perfect in design. No roots, no stems, just the importance of brightness that attracts a buyer of these fabrics to arrange them without vases, and put them on duvets.

The warmth of breaking bread at the table with cheerful borders; and pillows that one comforts one's back with, or covers one's over-fat belly with, or hides the rising warmth behind zippers.

Pillows that are bordered with brightness so that one awakens with the crow of the cock and knows there is sun for the day and gives us happiness that is wrapped in a paisley shawl with all those little similar paisleys reminding us of the feudal system; all alike in pattern.

Let us be well-spaced that there is a sense of congruity, a sense of well-being that socialism can be the same as capitalism when we are cheerful in those Provencal furnishings of France that do not fragment, but integrate an energy field without stipulations and definitions.

Concubine

i knew it was going to be a very difficult day as i pulled
on my L.L. Bean boots, tucked my sagging *breasts* into
my athletic bra, took a bit of 'Coming Up Roses'
lipstick for the outline of my mouth that might utter
words that i didn't mean all day, and then went
dutifully downstairs to the right wing of the house and
tried to read the Sunday paper sitting beside the
warrior husband i try to live with.

Of course his war now occurs in the business world
and because we are in business as equal partners it
occurs to me that we are not a mounted front but
offense and defense.

i have been in business for thirty-five years and after
his retirement from the military he came into the
business and has been there for fifteen years. We have
made good investments together, and now he is trying
to destroy them. The reason being that epidemics take
place. The problem is that if you let a child have too
much freedom, let Alabama man have too much
freedom, allow men like my husband to have too
much midnight lemonade, they turn into howling
wolves hungry for every prey, not simply what is in
their path.

So we went far and wide, innocent and aristocratic,
to find a whore; a whore for money. i guess i never
knew what a whore was. i guess i never thought about

them at all except in cowboy movies when they wore lace stockings and the cowboys had been on very long rides with cattle and conquered men in saloons. This need, i now realize, is very normal.

i guess i never called that fruit gathering.

Well, we had this woman who gathered a lot and she was 1990 vintage. She was miserably unhappy, consequently spreading her miseries into every part of my life: business, family, friendships and anything else that was my own.

So for these past fifteen years my life has been juggled and buffeted by people without purpose, emotionally restricted, emotionally dependent, demanding without giving, engulfed in an exaggerated sense of self-importance, offering little, taking much, and in the wake of their being remains a void and a despair that becomes unbearable. The void and despair were frequently salvaged by filling them with the golden liquid from the Chevas Regal bottle.

So it has been fifteen years of making money in the slough of despondence.

This intruder would not respond except to the colonel. She reached into the depths of his pockets until they were empty, and he constantly refilled them.

She wielded her mastery to control everything we had built for twenty-five years. She wanted its power, she wanted to use it.

However this story cannot be told, because there is plenty of violence in his bones, but there are widely publicized recommendations for families who…

Insanity

For Taylor Gates Blackwell it was a typical Sunday morning. The early morning sun was shining through the window in her 'reclaimed room'. It had been the room of Taylor's daughter, but the daughter had left her room, her town, even her country, to find life with the man she loved. The daughter now lives in the Netherlands, his home, now hers. Taylor rejoices in having this room. It will be what Virginia Woolf calls, 'a room of one's own'. Something Taylor has never had. Briefly perhaps, for a moment, but she always lost it, given to one more deserving, or so she was made to think. Masochism? Maybe.

As quietly as possible, Taylor tiptoes down the stairs, hoping to prevent any noise that will surely awaken her boisterous husband. She puts that off as long as she can.

Taylor's husband sleeps in the right wing of the house. It is the brown room of the right wing. It is his alone. He is an only child. Son of the military; his father, a career army officer, rising to the rank of colonel. Taylor's husband was a career army officer also; he too rose to the rank of colonel. He prefers to be called 'Colonel'. His parents adored him thinking he bore within him a touch of God. Did they really know him?

This suite of rooms is also occupied by the Spinster Spain, who, for no good reason, took up residence with the Blackwells many years ago. Her stay was to be brief, just until her health improved. She has never recovered, at least not well enough to go home.

She is very old. She is both brilliant and insane. She has a personality disorder the therapist calls 'illusions of grandeur'. Brilliance and insanity feed the disorder.

In Taylor's mind she has given the suite a name. It is 'Insanity'.

Unfortunately another inhabitant shares the suite. A bulldog by the name of 'Abigail'.

As a puppy, from her genetic line of inheritance, her acquired genius was evident. But she is a prisoner in the right wing. The right wingers from 'Insanity' use her to fulfill their emptiness and aloneness. She is both possessed and abused, petted and kicked, pampered and yelled at and denied all rights to freedom. My husband's abuse turns this well-bred animal into a despoiler of oriental rugs. The spinster declares her to be dehydrated and subsequently gives her shots of saline solution to ease her discomfort. She is dehydrated in purpose. Abigail bears the brunt of dehydration in purposelessness.

As Taylor descends the stairs, she can hear the faint snoring of her son. He is such a kind soul, she thought, even in his sleep she could hear his breathing, like the light, soft sounds of classical music, like that which comes forth from our state-of-the-art stereo, which on occasion would work. (In an eleven thousand square foot house maintenance is the constant.) The Blackwells managed to have a work crew, Rastafarians in appearance, which claimed to be correcting the failures, but the results were nefarious.

Looking out of the window, Taylor saw what seemed to a be ghostly gleam appear across the frost. She noticed there were only three cars sitting in her driveway. This was most unusual. The rate of traffic exiting and entering her driveway was five cars per hour every twelve hours. For partial use of the property, the Blackwells received a tax deduction. This home standing here is nothing more than a lovely furnished hotel meeting room. Family, to her husband, is his business. Therefore real family does not exist.

Taylor is startled to see how orderly the yard looks with just three Mercedes parked in the driveway. Usually her husband insists on parking vans and vehicles all over the yard, on the plants or on the newly landscaped areas. He argues, 'The more vehicles, the more business, the more money to spend on landscaping.' His logic is senseless.

Her son, philosophically, is a staunch defender of individualism. If he were to awaken, mother and son would nod condolences and in so doing know that silently, midst all the grandeur and beauty of this posh neighborhood; Benzes, swimming pools, tennis courts, they live in a theater of the absurd.

Having forgotten that people accept niceties or trade deficiencies for values, she felt like an unrestrained figure with an absolute commitment to traditional forms again.

He is a very successful man, the husband that is. But, Reader, you know this. Words like tennis court, Benz (the biggest and best), swimming pool, posh; they all tell of success. To him that is all that matters. His tunnel vision toward purpose causes him to be a vulgar, uninteresting, sordid person to live with, hunt with, fish with, party with, have children with; do anything with, except work.

The business belongs to Taylor. She owns it, but his name is etched in marble, stone and bronze, wherever possible. She tries very hard to work with him. Her suggestions about taxes, ledger sheets, office staff, budgets, profits, losses, whether calmly spoken, or sometimes shouted, sometimes whispered, usually fall on deaf ears.

He is a great sales person. He knows it and acts like a god. He has replaced Taylor with his love of selling.

She is lonely. She buys a lot of scotch.

They are like two buzzards who feed off one another's carrion.

Taylor is striving to make changes. She is, in a sense, maturing. In her loneliness she goes so far as to consider life with another woman, or having one of those same-sex marriages.

She knows that would mean divorce. She knows even the thought of divorce would destroy her husband. He loves his family, so he says.

Taylor feels like a prisoner, a prisoner bound by commitment. She is a shell which has no life within it. What else is there to life?

Yet, she says she will not be vulnerable. 'Absolutely not!'

Again, she looks across her lawn and rather than the beautiful boxwoods, gone with her husband's extensive pruning, she sees U-Hauls, trucks, vans, Mercedes, sometimes tomato stakes, and chickens. That is his life.

She feels the wonderful silence of a Sunday morning. She knows she can make silence.

Barefooted, she runs along the driveway to retrieve the bulk load of papers this 'insane' household demands. They all fight over the paper because they all want the same section at the same time. Everyone in this house envisions himself as part of the privileged class. Being an only child or a spinster, one never had to share.

She picks up the *Nashville Tennessean*, four to be exact, and the *New York Times*. The *Times* was a gift from a friend. She and her friend thought if they read that paper they could discuss world affairs rather than constantly and fruitlessly discussing children.

She is panting as she reaches the front door and gleefully dances up the stairway, realizing that no one is awake. At the top of the stairs, she turns like a frightened doe who has escaped the hunter by skillfully running through ponds, leaping over the barbed wire fence into the shadows the trees make and becoming a part of the landscape.

Ironically, she looks back into the clearing of the mist-covered meadow knowing inherently that this is a paradox of freedom. Did she not always know the expert hunter sat perched in the clearing, in a shining where not so well hidden deer stand? She is numbed by the thought that makes a mockery of her. The hunter makes the perfect shot.

Suddenly, she is stunned by the unbelievable thought that she is part of the network!

Didn't her husband always park cars in his mother's yard and didn't his father always park trucks in the yard of her dream house in Birmingham? The one she was promised after twenty long years of military service. Didn't his father always keep his dogs not in the kennel, but in the garage, that magic garage that had a magic door-opener? In fact, didn't those dogs always sleep next to the cabinet she had built to store extra food for when they got old, or where she would store food for parties, for friends; the friends who never came, the parties they never had? Didn't her husband and his father both plant tomatoes in the iris beds?

She glanced back through the French doors and laughed at herself midst the silence of this Sunday morning. She had been tricked!

Yesterday, she had allowed her son and his friend to build a portable duck blind that was hidden behind the first spring forsythia, and the camper top of his Ford pickup was wedged against a rather well-disguised dog kennel she had built for the dog.

She had always thought of herself as a business woman, a mother, philanthropist, entrepreneur, poet, tennis player. She really never thought of herself as failing to recognize what was evident; liking women better than men or being a wild woman.

She looks down at the headlines of the paper. The article concerns women who are angry because of the two failed nominations for the attorney general appointment. Taylor sighs, maybe women don't deserve to become attorney generals under Clinton.

The illegal alien issue was the cause, she thinks to herself. Husbands don't take responsibility for domestic affairs, they just leave it all to women. This sounds backhanded. Woman don't work. They bear children. They provide the XX vs the XY chromosome in the female/male genetic pattern. As a result, in evolution they produced a defective female in a great desire to mirror themselves.

Insanity!

January Apparition
(for Cecil Elrod, Jr.)

The frost spills snow on to the hedges.

i look down Main Street at foggy street lamps.

My father lived here, and his father and his father and a friend of his father.

But love was inherited through whiskey.

i remember his red face and pale eyes, his articulate words that rambled behind a dirty bow tie and soiled shirt.

Somewhere he promised me love.

We were both born in January.

He loved music from the heart, i learned that music is love.

We ever drink.

To Adrienna (A Fixed Perspective On Love)

Elizabeth heard them grandfathered like clauses in tax reforms. Like her grandmothers who sat with parasols and held their hands across their breasts.

Elizabeth did not say this. i did.

i hear them grandfathered like clauses in tax reforms. My grandmothers who sat with parasols and held hands across their breasts in favor of women's vote.

i look at you and we blend into pink and white cotton candy shirts with polo emblems.

We have always unconsciously touched.

i used to long for your round body, now thinner.

Now, i make a synonym of a face, fragile and frail, that needs my strength.

You shared your secrets like a sister.

All those years, like chambered nautili, we slept in separate rooms.

All these years, a winning championship tennis match, kiss, or brief handshake made me wild with passion.

Who were you to say no to a common language of need and drug me with margaritas?

We played Pictionary or Trivial Pursuit with the competition of lovers.

We satirized pathetic characters in Anne Tyler's books.

Drank bottles of wine instead of making love.

You, the calligrapher of silence etching 'no', 'no', 'no', to me.

We used postcards for love notes, 'Wish you were here'.

i am in love with Picasso and lavender.

We posed inanimate in photos.

Brief embraces of 'hellos', and 'goodbyes', like self-conscious children reciting poetry in front of the class.

But, no one was watching.

Conservative passion all these years.

You could have left; remarried.

The terms are shorter now, like some fixed asset.

The community sees us together, living next door to one another.

'Good neighbors,' they say.

One day my dog was killed,

the one we walked in the park.

The third party you said was, 'Only an animal'.

They found me hanging by his leash in the garage.

Such a tragedy. Her best friend found her.

'They were such good neighbors.'

i know you read the note tearlessly each night, and tuck it away in the brown file.

You never told them there was a note.

Part Two

Exchange of Thoughts With a Poet Friend

Just Like Daddy
Pipecutters

Tom,

Have you read *Stained Glass* by Rosanna Warren? It is
very good and dry and i think her poetry is in perfect
poetic form. She is a friend's friend.
Would you like the book?
Or should i study it?

You know i will not,

Karen
January 1995

Dear Tom,

This mind appreciates your considering my mind for the course; the presentation was non-sequential because i needed to send you something, to get back something that would give me a lifeline to go on; like the telephone is an umbilical cord for failing sixty-five year old businessmen, and artists who must suffer solitude but have to speak, to agitate, to start battle, to defend and offend until they have no friends to call behind their hallucinations of failure. They have won at battle and there is no one left to fight, so they die under their defensive Southern pride and are cremated or wrapped in the shroud of a Confederate flag with the circle showing one star, that significant one star; that one star to symbolize what was to have been a nation.

Die hard Southerner.

Die
hard
Southerner.

Tom,

Your handwriting is romantic with its little slants of
wisdom, your blue ink reminds me of 'blue moon',
'standing alone there', your comments are first-class to
a second-class mind; i am not deprived or anything,
you should see the wonderful social and financial
accolades i have received; and all i want is a rainbow
with all the colors and, at the end, a blending of color
to make me over.

i even saw a perfect rainbow last month and tried to
make the sequence of colors into a primary color
picture so i could understand a painting i had seen;
assuming God and artists mix their own colors and
make wonderful presentations. Well, i could not
remember the sequence even though i saw five distinct
colors, i mixed and got black and i wonder if that was
what God was looking for and you are probably saying,
by this far into reading the line, 'Fuck you, Tennessee
trash'. i have tried you with Pablo Neruda and Emily
Dickinson and with Tom McKeown in a wheelchair
hanging on, not by asparagus hearts but asparagus
strings that have been chewed and eaten, digested and
fornicated, and i cannot get your strength.

Tom,

i like your stationary and general casualty because i am generally never going to submit or give up; you should see that now i write and now i paint wildflowers to illustrate talk about 'hymn to the marvelous'. The painting is much worse than the writing but my children think it is good; not much of a comparison.

So now i have lashed out at you; understood Robert Bly, had dinner for breakfast since i forgot to eat last night, had a ten thousand dollar day, drank one scotch and water before five, and watched *Even Cowgirls Get the Blues*. i guess i will go to the dry cleaners and get my son's girlfriend's coat that the black lab slept on on Christmas Eve, see if i can think of anything for three Black-related household domestics to polish or cook, or just let them drink my Chevas Regal so i can get out and buy some more, make a few calls in my PMS state, that can range from outrageous to seductive and embarrass a few people. It is (Feluda's) Backlash i pattern myself after, watch a French film with subtitles, try to learn about Windows on my computer (i just put more windows up for fresh air and don't get the oxygen).

i talk to a family member, check the frozen pipes in a grandiose old 1870 Italianate villa, a Southern home, a dream house built by a Southern general and now held by a Southern 1990s woman, argue with the

Spinster Spain, who i took in out of compassion when she was sick and who has lived here for seventeen years. i call the geriatric psychiatrist about her which will then send her back to changing her will, accept a smoked turkey from my Black courier, who has had a heart attack and confused my book-keeper, Elnora, with my maid, Magnolia, (euphonious). He was trying to get a screw out of Magnolia, and Elnora received the turkey because of wrong name labeling, so now he has to smoke another turkey. Maybe he will label more carefully next time.

She likes Wild Turkey anyway.

Well if you made it this far, Tom, don't you feel sorry for me.

What am i torturing you for?

i think you have a brain that delivers messages.

i think you have an illuminous revolver that lies on your chest, across your heart and will pull the trigger when it is time.

Thanks,
Karen.

Tom,

i am trying to come up with titles for a non-sequential, Southern tragedy (chap) book; i am thinking like writing:

Archeological Ruins That Mother Ate

(with lots of big white columns on the cover of the book, all overturned and sideways and with Southern hairstyles and lots of teeth)
    or:

Daddy Built A Sand-Castle
But Too Late

  or:

Daddy Built A Sand Castle Lost To The Tides

(Inside acknowledgment.)
    What am i but me: a Civil War 'mutant', who sits on the porches of old houses rocking with skeletons in peeling, painted rockers; sitting on back porches, i told old Bone he was Black; and that there was a White dame from town who loved him, that the Civil War was over; it was 1995, and the millennium war was his.

Tom,

i have four more 'Pipecutter poems' and ten more 'Just
Like Daddy' and some 'Decadent South' poetry.
    I AM TOUR OF HOMES in the deep South
    NOT ALL THE HOMES HAVE BEEN SHOWN by request
or they are 'Not For Sale'.

    i see this evolving into prose poetry.

Part Three
Bare Bones Journal

May 20

i am so very tired of caring. Salvation should render itself soon. i want to have a day when dependents miss me with joy. How did my little Catherine develop removal without loneliness, i do not understand. Elizabeth and Jackson are seen more often coming and going with great airs of confidence and independence so that there is no obligation to the stately mansions that made them such lofty individuals. None of these uncompromising inheritors, with attitude or cultural change, mind breaking any wall the bastions created for them.

i have to remember that in a psychology study the baby ducks followed a vacuum cleaner instead of their mother which indicates to me that what passes for love is merely a rudimentary kind of object attachment.

None of my children will compromise their inheritance. They will not compromise attitude or cultural change or part with any bastion they might inherit.

They like the attitude and culture of turnip stems, black-eyed peas, magnolias and have expectations of all women becoming CEOs. They cherish heart pine floors, fourteen-foot ceilings, and large houses but refuse to live in them. Bastion?

May 21
Feminists' Fury: Unchambered, Naked Nautilus II

First off, my deliberation on feminists is from the background of a small town girl who lived the myth of what a good little girl should be in all of the literal, traditional translations until she was nineteen... then, no matter what parents or teachers or friends said, there was almost an immediate adult chrysalis, but tarnished.

As i make entries into this journal, which started as a short story, i laugh at the names of the specimens of butterflies i have caught today; and find an hysterical resemblance to my own life: for instance, what if the Goatweed Emperor bred with the Painted Lady and ended up with a Puss Moth Larvae? the not so nice analogies that fall out about the inbred Southern eccentrics. Anyway, the chrysalis of the Goatweed Emperor has spent her short nineteen-year life unhappily hanging on the side of politeness, sweetness, and obedience, clinging to the East Main Street house, and then emerging like a Goatweed Emperor (Capricorn, she is) with flaming colors for a short flight until she makes a reflection of her mother (a battle ax in her own right), this emotionally poverty-stricken repetition finds a US colonel to marry.

Now the predecessors, the forebears, as well as offspring of this species, literally eat themselves out of house and home. When their food is so chewed and bitten to pieces that there is not enough left for the next generation to pull around to weave silk or gold, they simply find another leaf close by. This species also hibernates when degrees drop.

Following thru with this story, this almost nineteen year old adult grew into an exceptional-looking but mainstream butterfly, that really was more like a Monarch (an early emergence of brilliance) than an Emperor. The Monarch is the strongest flier. These great butterflies are migratory, but only to the south. Luxurious food keeps them from becoming established in Europe and other continents. Even though their migratory routes deviate, from time to time, they always return to the South.

There are even Viceroys who mimic Monarchs, which we will take up later.

So old bone, where did it start? Maybe in Tennessee, maybe in England on the Henson side, maybe just in Tennessee. My people on all sides, whoever or whatever they think they are, they just migrated to the hills of Tennessee.

Well, i don't like Richard Wilbur and all of that: but i told ole bone that i could have dreams every night about the things he had lived and so often the things are enough.

i kind of fondled an old hearth broom, one that my grandmother had given me or, i asked for in an estate divide because i liked it and always remembered Grandnana's story about how she picked it up in an antique shop and that their fireplace never worked on Brainard Road in Chatanooga. In fact, it was out of style since most of those people had just moved into new houses in the Twenties with coal furnaces. It was a big jump from hauling wood to having a man come and fill up the coal bin, and my grandfather could just put it in a stoker.

Did i tell you about the gold knife papa gave me when i was six and his furnace that was electric?

But that is a deeper process than this broom my grandmother never used, because one day i read where it was made by Berea College, Student Industrial Project, Berea, Kentucky.

Well, i always thought it was a secret that my beloved Grandnana had not gone to college, but i probably knew she hadn't because the only travel she had ever mentioned was with Aunt Connelly who lived in Tampa, Fla. or maybe Miami, Fla.

But they found all of these wonderful fighting conch shells and she told me Aunt Connelly collected shells and actually those were her inheritance because i took care of Nana in her last years and i knew.

She loved my children and hated me at the end, even tried to have me arrested because i took her gun.

That was supposed to protect 'Hunna' – that was Grandfather's affectionate name for her.

When they were richer they had a second house. It was a cabin on Chickmauga Lake without running water.

And i loved it since our family had played trick economics and we had bigger houses and bigger cars than Grandnana but i still loved Grandnana who loved me.

June 1

There are even Viceroys who mimic Monarchs which we will take up later.

The early-bloomer teenager sells herself successfully to the public of her town as an entrepreneur: a child prodigy in business and a woman of the late Fifties who was of machismo primogenital inheritance. That inheritance being a ladies' department store (less capital). Thus name only. There were six (male) figures associated with the business before (way before), since many Emperors, Monarchs, and Viceroys existed before; not necessarily in royal order.

Kind, cordial, taste to purchase for the wealthy, bright enough on the left side of the brain to be a leader, this young girl worked with her seventy-five year old grandfather, then started a business of her own. Was adored by her small town and became almost instantly successful. Bookkeeping skills were not as apparent as salesmanship, as she hired the family bookkeeper who was working for Grandfather (and who had a criminal record), used her grandfather's over ages of inventory, which she craftily merchandised (and smuggled out the back door) in repayment for the money her grandfather took from her profits when she worked for him: (cyclic enough) which he had also taken from her father; his own son. The Monarch saved money in her swift flight to success and clothed her four siblings as any daughter turned mother, not by choice but by demand, would. She rose above her mother with this monetary success. Scepter. Her mother was held high. Then a jealousy of becoming child was raging and warlike for the rest of her mother's life. And there was the alcoholic father who loved her but lived in alternating fogs of reality. Being the brother's keeper to his father. A resigned bottle of lemon oil polish was what little aristocracy the family had during social events.

The undercurrents of this well-educated father (Georgia Military Academy) which was still (stratigizing) for Sherman in 1920 and Vanderbilt Frat brother who swigged gin in between winning high rums and distance runs and attending the Davis cup finals: repeating Eddie Mims Shakespeare and moving his six foot five frame with the gracefulness of Nijinsky, once professing to be Diaghilev. But he was dutifully called back home after having been missing in action for three years (Palm Beach sporting goods owner and financier Cecil Elrod) to be called to active duty by a good cousin who was also Secretary of State, actively became Brazil's darling of the tennis circuit and sometimes radar engineer for the US Army. Gallantly, it was his voice that announced the war was over with a deep resonance, a beautiful articulation as long as it was at a radio station behind a microphone. This led to the return of the hometown boy to start the State of Tennessee's first radio station in his father's building with his father's money. (The demise.)

So his first-born monarch-to-be endured life until flight. Her first journey across the street from her family home, that address being 1153 East Main: she traveled afar to 1150 East Main.

Crippled in spirit, this father saw hope for a return on his money in his daughter, and a relationship he had always sought, you might say even a reflection. Calculatingly, he supported his daughter as he traveled in a triangle between 934 East Main, 1153 East Main, 1150 East Main, and much later this child prodigy turned feminist, not Christ-like, home 924 East Main.

This daddy labored over theories and talked of long-deceased socialites and sport celebrities such as Bobby Riggs and Patti Berg, Jimmy Connors, and Ivan Lendl, who were coming into stardom. He had lived before his time in saying industry would ruin the South; in fact he and the chamber were the first to bring industry to our small town; these Yankees being lured to the South by the fact that there was still a South with gentlemen who did not work, danced in the marble sunrooms and had cocktail hour, as a ritual, at 5 p.m. to discuss the progress of their town and national and international news. That there were grand homes run by Black staff, and always a well-kept steel magnolia as a wife and hostess, who served a formal dinner at 8 p.m., long after these gentlemen had retired in a stupor of alcoholic slumberland to enter the next day with bloody marys and patterns of unkept grandeur. Dinner was served.

A project from war days was understanding wiring better than utility companies and taking the children's telephone from an upstairs bedroom to the new merchant who might be the monetary salvation of the family. Cleverly, he strung yards of wire among squirrels' nests and mocking birds' songs into the new store, no commercial rates for this daughter's first venture, costing only the family's party line conversations over customer calls. This was a male chauvinist with a real umbilical cord to all the children's lines number 1945. The cord was never cut and today at fifty-one the number is attached to his daughter and her business. History proves it with AT&T.

As i type, my seventy-five year old mother calls to ask what she should wear to my daughter's graduation, and if i am writing to be sure and write nice poetry.

There is something wonderfully evil about being inbred and close and buying the finest mansion in town, down from Daddy's.

Meeting a militarist leader after all the Southern gentleness was exciting, but not insightful. Not recognizing the reflection of Mother in the guise of hard-core love and sex and after having a very brief affair with Dad. This Dagger Moth colonel who fed on cottonwoods was in the guise of an Imperial or was a Common White. First of all the Common White lays its eggs in or on other insects that will later serve as food. Incorrect, the ichneumon fly is the one who does that, the Common White uses ants to protect its young by mixing sperm as sweet as honey which ants feed on and will protect under any conditions.

The Imperial is yellow like the father but wears illusory armor and could be mistaken for another lepidopterous insect because of its imposing presence.

The Imperial or Common White assumed the Cadillac had a chauffeur, that his sought-after Monarch would have never smoked a cigar or drunk whiskey or made love to the local circuit judge who was a homosexual. She always wore Bermuda shorts, from knee to foot being her most shapely feature, then a tucked, white starched shirt, a cameo with gold filigree, an heirloom and weejuns. A great athlete, golden hair and stubbornness was enough to catch a Common White or an Imperial Colonel off guard. The colonel used to explain ambush tactics to this vintage Vougette and her insides would tickle, some emotional restraint stopping that laughter from becoming reality.

(These boots were made for walking and i will walk all over you or my father. i'll have it my way.)

i am still working on the short story i conceived the first morning.

May 22

Some thoughts first. Sarah N. who is such a lovely, thoughtful person invited me to play tennis. My back was tight but the company was so enjoyable. She is an attribute to the social fabric of the world, respecting everyone's beliefs and is not intimidated. She is truly a justice to one's ego, and never will turn back.

Now for the ailing back. It hurts but I get by well.

Believing in lack of stress, relief from menses, a bit of tennis and alignment and assurances from Zana, Roberta and my faithful confidant, Cynthia. Perhaps even the typewriter that works to express my regrets that we live by a 'Newtonian' clock in a rational and objective world. i still believe that absolute time is not the measuring stick for all biological phenomena. From Stephen Gould the (bamboo canes) wait a hundred and twenty years before flowering again. Humpback whales memorize thirty minute songs, birds migrate: deer know their rutting season, jet lag is the price we pay for moving faster than time. Thank you, Stephen Gould, the 'mayfly' lives a day as an adult, we have days upon end. Let us not waste them.

Karen read Robert Chambers' *The Vestiges of Natural History of Creation* 1844; pre-Darwin.

Betty Rollin so ably said that if God were still speaking to us in a voice we could hear, even he would probably say be fruitful, don't multiply, but the town prodigy multiplied and had three little strands of worry beads around her neck for twenty-five years. These little nooses that were not heavy, but colorful, and served as beautiful ornamentation for Mother. Then through wear and age the strands broke, fell from Mother's neck and became the most creative, fruitful adults.

Each child gathered their little orbital ideas and became one huge planet; not little frail Southern agrarian aristocrats sucking on hind tits, but great orbital planets that entered a world of reality where women occasionally did not want to marry, where women were equal to men, where color of skin did not matter and a young man could have the blushing admission behind football helmets and cleats and coaches awards that he was a poet and an artist.

Socialization began to play a part in this great society and the Monarchs managed to migrate to the European continent, where they will hopefully develop a strong propensity for the gusto of living.

Part Four

Verse

Self-Portrait of a Daughter

Expand a memory from
flushing anger into a powered cheek,
Calm, wicked, sweet, passive,
with venom that crouches, watering in the larynx,
watering, waiting to strike.
This mother, this masochist,
beating herself frail.
Trying to hide.

Circumflexes appear on her body
the eyes, the cheeks, the head,
all alike, half circles in sacrifice.

Prismatic against the dark circles,
her breasts droop for suckle,
by man, by child, by friend, all unweaned.
The emerging milk dribbles over the crucifix,
the heaving breasts crushing the sternum,
the cross that is covered with bulging life,
the heave, the rhythm like an abacus counting;
clinking, clicking, clicking,
counting time until it is gone.

Lately, she makes shadows of her own face,
there is energy subtracting her heart from her soul.
There is no sound, no measure.
The bosoms droop over the cavern
that has always remained empty.

Her body like a round ball of symmetrics
becoming only a head;
a female face to live on a wall
of self-portraits of courageous,
dismembered martyrs,
whose voices have whispered in crescendos
that have never been heard.

Waiting for the Streetcar
Canvas Kid (Homeless Woman in Tennis Shoes)

i sleep on a concrete bench
in the summer heat,

Watching foreign cars
make silver streaks of paved roads.

Three-breasted suits flash by
reciting Yiddish.

At this hour
the metro stops with a toxic screech.

As i step aboard,
the crowd becomes one wrinkled face,
the brown vinyl sticks to my dress.

i take a bread sack of leftovers
and share with Jack.
He will get off at Main and Broad
to fuck the wino's wife.

She is his bed of summer zinnias
hardy, colorful, but still
thirsting for water to survive.

Oh, Marigold If You Were Only Here

i read you last night in a book as a child of healing.
Now i feel the rock child: the child of kneeling.
A friend of mine has a song
'In Other Words', there are no words.
Have you thought of words that they never were,
but in the expression of a flight of a butterfly;
in the hopping of a rabbit in a field.

A return on being human, to account for words at all;
how unhappy can a man be,
how afraid of women in love with men?
Back to the old word; i like androgyny
in other words; if there were no words
Marigold, you would still be here;
and poor, old rock woman, slug woman, would profit
by no speech at all.

A Child of Many

One never knows a child of many,
you are pushed, you have narratives that are not your
  own;
you might be thinking, and the aura of the family
  might think you're laughing.
You might really be into heavy things,
and your family thinks there is lightness of being;
your mother might think chocolate is your favorite
  flavor,
when peppermint ice was the only thing.
You might like to feel the family room alone,
and they all come crashing in, (wondering what silence
  is).
You might say green and mean
the mossy stuff on the farmer's pond,
and your mother thinks of Christmas trees with
  shining tinsel;
you might have a script all of your own but it goes
  unsaid
because you are stunned by interruptions of things said
  better;
dutiful, you wait your turn, and then you run.

Life as a child of many makes you a vagabond;
a vagabond with lots of color; a cliché, an old hat
that has never been worn.
So, run vagabond, and make the noise that is all your
    own.

I Keep Things Forever

i keep things forever, i never let go.
Like my best high school friend who went to Harvard,
i went to Tennessee Tech.
We scored the same on the SATs.

i keep things forever,

like my maid Magnolia, who loves me as a friend.
She has Alzheimer's and an alcoholic pancreas and i
    still let her come and pretend she cooks and house
    cleans and pay her a thousand dollars a week
    because we have both developed bad habits of
    spending the money we make on the best products.
Hers, the finest country hams at seventy dollars a
    pound, and gold leaf mirrors Southern families find
    cumbersome.
Mine, Outward Bound trips, and skiing trips and
    hunting trips,
and Patagonia outer wear, Cabelas duck calls, rifles
    with Zeiss scopes and European vacations,
and jewelry; a box of pearls, five thousand dollars,
    worn once a year with hunting clothes, a tennis
    outfit, or maybe to a funeral.

i keep things forever,

like the therapist who is going in the opposite
    direction.
She has an adopted child, she is forty-three,
my confidante for many years.
She is now changing diapers.
i had children at twenty-three.
i go white-water rafting with a daughter of twenty.

i keep things forever,

like driving to Cody, Wyoming with my nineteen year
    old son who now drinks Jim Beam.
He goes with eight guides to the mountains to hunt
    and
i wait at the ranch, praying for his safe return.
i become the medicine woman, i pray at the foot of the
mountain.

Hearing the real Black Foot River run through it,
my spirit rides the clouds,
but nowhere close to heaven.
i return to the ranch and the old cowboy conveniently
    shows up at cocktail time and tells me the tall tales
    of the day.
i am spiritually drawn to this soother of pain.

i keep things forever,

like Janet Frame's 'Diviners' or 'Angel at My Table'. i
cling to this attachment like it is the only realization
i have ever had of child abuse.

The Pipecutters
A Category for Women
Chant
(Fitting Into a White Male System)

i began to understand the system
as my children learned to lace their shoes.
i began to understand the system
as i drove my children off to school.
i began to envy men. Where were the roses?
Where was the love?
Where was the friend?
Why was i called the fucking whore?
When i was a wife, a Mother and much more.

The children grew in whole circles,
and i was still a half.
Those wholes reflected me less a woman,
more a man.
Subtracting all the marriage, tribal things
i beat my chest and used all power plays with jobs and
    friends.
Then came home to emptiness.
No one is hungry anymore. No one is sick. No one
    suffers.

i left my mansion for a cottage in the woods.
i left three adults filled with values of androgyny,
the wholeness with which they ought to live.

i am a pipecutter on the sewer lines
And write poetry every day.
My hard hat protects me while i work.
Little do my fellow men know the joy i am acting out,
Cutting all the lines, making fittings with whitish
    caulk,
(reminding me of white shoe polish,
reminding me of heavy starch on sheets).

Each time the foreman yells 'cut twenty feet of line', i
    cut fifty.
i smell the sewer draining a sweet and rancid smell.

He would never understand, the big white man,
he would never understand a woman cutting pipelines.
Pipedreams.

He yells orders, eats his lunch and wants a fuck,
and i am a pipecutter, cutting line.
A workman just to fit the foreman's screws.
But he will never understand the joy i feel.
He cannot understand.
He yells out twenty; i cut fifty,
Everyday.
And it is not his way…

You know we are one and many,

staggering around the mockery of men.

We are thick with a mother's pain

and strangled by a sub-gender of our father's sin.

We are the rebels with the flag,
although tattered and torn,

underskirting the knights of round
with the analogy of the square divide.

The Pipecutter's Chant

i said i was the pipecutter
letting rain beat upon my hat.
Orders are to lay fifty by the day,
i can lay two thousand by the month.
Rain or shine the job is done.
i am one of forty pipecutters.
There are only ten today because of weather.
Five females tow the rope.
Five females seal the joints with caulk.
The rain is mixed with salty tears
across my face.
This job is too hard, hatred, anger,
hostility drive me on.

We break for lunch.
The men lying close together under the knarled oak,
laughing about the latest sexist joke.
The women drenched in white coarse shirts
with names written across their breasts,
indicating they belong to the pipecutter's union
and have a name. The lacy bras are a dead giveaway
that they are seconds.

Chant III

i am trying to say i can't get the writer and the
conformist to separate.
i can't get the paper and the typewriter together.
i can't get 'loving you' on tape.
i can't get the pipecutters to quit cutting.

i think the pipecutters remember who they are
but their hats have changed,

like they had a cranial or something
in neuromuscular therapy.
The kind of therapy where you don't do a lot
of talking about your past history
and about your friendships.
But the kind of therapy where you undress,
like naked, in front of these people
and they pull on your hair and your head and it
brings up memories.
The reason you undress fully and stay under a
sheet is to feel vulnerable.

They never address your body,
just your head and pull your hair,
like you were an angel who went to sleep, or
something like that.

And you have angel hair and they really awaken
all the things in your system.
That's what a cranial is.

The Pipecutters' Chant IV

And when i say IV i mean
intravenous,
like real substance.
it's not easy to expect perfection, yet with all the
correction,
one might advocate the children get a friend before a
parent,
a CPA before a friend,
a dog before entering the desert alone.

No one knows why people turn away from the path
where all the primroses stand.
i know why i did that only remaining thing,
to sing my own song.
i sang a song of myself of twenty years ago,
and i sing it still again.
What shoe lies bare upon the soul and the toe is
mighty thin.
We pivot. We turn

and it's worn,
not fit to go another place
but to turn your wings like a cock about to fight.
It has nothing to do with your flight, it has to do with
your feet in your 'sharpless' spurs.
How far can they dig and how deep?

You asked me for another verse of pipecutters
but they are still trying to lay those pipes way down
    without a drainage point,

without thinking of primitive is a straight shoot.
i am a hunter
and my best man is my loot.
He died yesterday of cancer 'melanoma', they said.
No i'm sure it was the hills we did not climb.
He was my friend, Hal,
i spelled it Howell, like on his stone. But i am never
    alone.
The hell with Arlington.
He was the clear spring where the pipecutters now put
    their stuff.

i was aware that his mother was still alive
long after he died at fifty-eight and his father died at
    ninety-five, leaving his estate that
his daughter would tender until the box
would hold no more.
Then they gave it only to the poor.

So pipecutters
hit the line when it's hard.

Love your life while you are here. Don't be like the
    hen who plucks the yard after the rooster has been
    there.

They never hit a pipeline
or not very often.
They love to give their banter to a hen.
hit the lines cutters
the time is here.

i was asked to write this verse as a backwash
to sewage on the ground.
Find another, it goes on as it bubbles and we call the
    metro police,
who prick the concrete like it was mud
and i think of concrete being hard.

Hit pipecutters, it's your union and without clear
    drainage it's a nuisance.

Chant V

So the pipecutters get the line again.

Well, i had a pipecutter who went to Saint Mary's in
   North Carolina where they still talk about gender of
   alumnae, alumni and alumnus, whatever the Latin
   all pertains to.
But being a female is a real big deal in an Episcopal
   environment of the Carolinas.

Well, the female priest or priestess gets up and talks in
   gender.
Then the administrator of the school gets up at
   parent's day in the chapel, and talks about gender.
But they are all talking about alumni, alumnae,
   alumnus, like it really matters who graduates from
   Saint Mary's.
Well, finally, after the third semester my daughter
   called and said how miserable this alumnae-i-us was
   and she was going to backpack around Europe and
   live in youth hostels,
and it would not cost much money except for the
   'Grateful Dead' tickets.

i said, 'All right, i think you need a break.
As long as you go back and become an alumni,
   alumnae, alumnus deal.'

Guess what. i have an alumna magna cum laude!

Chant

All those pipecutters did for her was
set the line.
That example we look at on blueprints,
that blueprint we look at with blue bloods
who end up on the line to tow.
Go, woman, hit the pipeline,
the garbage will spew,
the time will fill the space,
just like Aunt Grace looking at old Uncle Henry
and going on down to the corner druggist
for morphine,
in 1913.

Go pipecutter, education will stay in remission
Until you find the meaning of
alumni, alumnae, alumnus.
Recently i noticed on the bottom of a pipe
that it was Japanese.

Symbiosis – Mothers to Daughters:

i have a great compassion, and care for you as a person.
The scenario is that you are addictive,
you promise me what i cannot give to myself
yet i cannot bear the pain for both of us in the
representation of birth and death
i feel like a painted friendship; a graffiti stage setting,
there is a villa that hides us behind stone walls
and we wander through gardens selecting flowers,
making colorful history of bouquets that we, ourselves,
have selected at random...
We meander all the unknown paths like regular
visitors.
There is a formality in the complexity of your face that
becomes interluding... i feel the resolution of my
own soul at war with a peacefulness;
i try to irrigate the landscapes with my tears; tears that
are so forced that they trickle into your trembling
hands,
your hands that draw the forced wetness, not like a
joyful measure,
but they are cupped disdainfully,
forming a vessel filled at an undesirable well...
Your hands have a leathery, worn, even tired
movement;
they do not like the artificial means of the water
supply;

your hands become uterine-like in shape; a narrow-mouthed container with depth...
Then the excitement that i might live or die through you evokes a brilliant color that is almost photostatic to the mind's i (eye).
An idiom of our friendship becomes mysterious;
i am forcing scripts and titles into your soul as if you were not my friend, but a costumed performer.
i am forever grateful that i cannot see you very well;
i would literally cling to a photograph; it would crumble beneath my intimidated fingers that now begin to turn intrepidly.
What beauty we have excavated from office visits,
you are like a coral reef with all the treasures that i have longed for:
islands, ships, villas, meandering walks, colorful bouquets with many specimens
have made my mental and physical relocation a possibility.
What an ambitious scheme for us both to be unsupportive;
unsuperficial;
the imaginary lines becoming so visible
that the dissolvement of friendship
is less painful
than the laborious task under which we strained to form one...

January Apparition
(for Cecil Elrod, Jr.)

The frost spills snow on to the hedges.

i look down Main Street at foggy street lamps.

My father lived here, and his father and his father and a friend of his father.

But love was inherited through whiskey.

i remember his red face and pale eyes, his articulate words that rambled behind a dirty bow tie and soiled shirt.

Somewhere he promised me love.

We were both born in January.

He loved music from the heart, i learned that music is love.

We ever drink.